No, because if I "drop it" you're just going to throw it again.

A third-string
pitcher is so
underappreciated.
Have you seen my
curveball?

I <u>do</u> love you. I'm just not ready to announce it to the world.

Wanna go outside? Let's go outside. Can we go outside? We should go outside. Have you been outside?

I don't care how much they paid for the couch. I slept on the old one and I'm sleeping on this one.

I won't tell
if you
won't tell.

Ever since I hurt my hip,
this is the only way I can keep up
with the mail carrier.

Blondes do
have more
fun.

Right now I'm doing your
typical puppy jobs, but what
I really want is to direct.

I have to walk
her twice a day.

My backside smiles so much,
my mouth doesn't have to.

I'll hide out
here until
they put the
two-year-old
to bed.

I may not be able to run anymore, but I'm wise enough to appreciate the days when I could.

I know I messed up, but people really need to realize they can't have nice things <u>and</u> a puppy.

Mrs. Johnson owns us all, so yeah, I guess that means we're related.

They
always say
they'll only
be a
minute.

I like the idea of a sandwich,
I've just never had the patience
to actually make one.

Can we do a picture with just the two of us? My ribs are killing me.

We have to go home now.
I need to call my broker.

I ran. I got the ball.
I brought it back.
Now what?

I wasn't worried until he started calling me his little McNugget.

Yeah, I ate the boy's homework. That's what I love to do, eat boys' homework.

Why do you guys think Mom's so happy all of a sudden?

No squirrel may pass.
I am the Squirrel Master.

Uh, you guys might want to sleep
downstairs tonight.

Pssst . . .
do you want to
know a secret?

I'm all ears.

Drop it. Drop it. Drop it.
Drop it. Come on, drop it.

This is torture. Someone call
the ASPCA.

You're definitely
picking the
wrong day to
mess with me.

Come to think of it, I probably should have opted for the money-back guarantee.

Come on now,
big girls
don't cry.

I can't believe we
have the same mother.

What obedience class? I was trained on the streets.

Sometimes I feel I'm a Jack Russell trapped in a bulldog's body. But then that goes away and I just sleep the rest of the day.

Don't look! I
haven't put on
my makeup yet.

I got my master's degree
from Barker College
and my Ph.D. from DePaw.

I only chewed up
one shoe. This seems like
a pretty steep sentence
for one lousy shoe!

Just leave _leave_ me alone,

would ya?

Just wanted to make sure you don't need any help. I'd be happy to help...really...just let me help!

I'm not tired. It's the ball that needs a rest.

This is where I nap. I
sleep in a king-size bed
with satin sheets and
fluffy pillows.

I'm telling you,
I'm not wearing the leash
in this family!

I thought I told her to upgrade me to first class!

What, me come there?
Why can't you come here
just this once?

The end.